Anne Frank

www.pegasusforkids.com

© **B. Jain Publishers (P) Ltd.** All rights reserved. No part of this book may be reproduced, stored in a retrieval system or transmitted, in any form or by any means, mechanical, photocopying, recording or otherwise, without any prior written permission of the publisher.

Published by Kuldeep Jain for B. Jain Publishers (P) Ltd., D-157, Sector 63, Noida - 201307, U.P
Registered office: 1921/10, Chuna Mandi, Paharganj, New Delhi-110055

Printed in India

Contents

5   Who was Anne Frank?

6   Early Life and Childhood

10   Time before Holocaust

17   Adolf Hitler

26   Hitler's Heartless Treatment of the Jews

30   The Franks' Hideout

40   Captured by the Nazis

44   The Diary of a Young Girl

49   Excerpts from the Diary of Anne Frank

60   Timeline

65   Activities

67   Glossary

Who was Anne Frank?

Anne Frank was one of the countless Jewish children who died in the holocaust. She was a German-Jewish teenager who was forced to go into hiding. She and her family, along with four others, spent over two years during World War II hiding in an annex of rooms above her father's office in Amsterdam.

Anne is today admired the world over for her style of writing in her diary, which she wrote during the Nazi invasion period. Her diary was later adapted into several plays and films. Since it was first published in 1947, Anne's diary has become one of the most powerful memoirs of the holocaust.

She was a German national by birth and remained so until 1941, when she lost her nationality due to the anti-Semitic policies during the Nazi Germany period.

Early Life and Childhood

Anne Frank, the remarkable young Jewish girl was born in Frankfurt, Germany on June 12, 1929. Daughter of Otto Frank and Edith Frank-Holländer, Anne had an elder sister, Margot Frank, who was born in the year 1926. Her family was of Jewish origin and they were quite liberal

in their outlook. They did not follow the conservative customs and traditions of Judaism. Anne was raised in a mixed community of Jewish and non-Jewish people.

Edith Frank was a dedicated mother, while Anne's father, Otto Frank, was more interested in scholarly pursuits than his children's upbringing. Otto Frank had an extensive collection of books in his library. Both the parents had one thing in common; both encouraged their children to read.

The Franks were a typical upper-middle class German-

Jewish family living in a quiet, religiously diverse neighbourhood near the outskirts of Frankfurt. However, Anne was born on the eve of dramatic changes in the German society that would soon disrupt her family's happy, tranquil life as well as the lives of all other German Jews.

Time before Holocaust

The term 'holocaust' is originally derived from the Greek word 'holokauston', which means 'sacrifice by fire'. It refers to the Nazis' persecution and planned slaughter of the Jewish people.

In addition to Jews, the Nazis targeted gypsies, homosexuals, Jehovah's Witnesses, and the disabled, for persecution. Anyone who resisted the Nazis was sent to forced

labour, or murdered. The term 'Nazi' is an acronym for 'Nationalsozialistishe Deutsche Arbeiterpartei' (National Socialist German Workers' Party).

After its defeat in World War I, Germany felt a sense of deep humiliation owing to the Versailles Treaty. Their pre-war territory and the armed forces were drastically reduced. The Allies demanded that Germany should acknowledge their responsibility for the outbreak of the war, and asked it to pay compensation to the allied powers.

With the German Empire destroyed, a new parliamentary government called the Weimar Republic was formed. The republic suffered from economic instability, which grew worse during the worldwide depression after the New York stock market crash in 1929. Massive inflation followed by very high unemployment rates heightened existing class and political differences, and began to undermine the government.

On January 30, 1933, Adolf Hitler, leader of the National Socialist German Workers (Nazi) Party, was named Chancellor of Germany by President Paul von Hindenburg after the Nazi Party won a significant percentage of votes in the elections of 1932. The Nazi Party had taken advantage of the political unrest in Germany to gain an electoral foothold. The Nazis incited clashes with the communists and conducted a ferocious propaganda campaign against

its political opponents—the weak Weimar government and the Jews whom the Nazis blamed for Germany's ills.

Realizing that under the power of the Nazis, the Jews in Germany were not safe, Otto Frank decided that his family should leave for some other country. In 1934, the family moved to the city of Amsterdam in the Netherlands. Anne was only four years old at that time. Before long, Anne had made new friends, was speaking Dutch, and was

going to school in a new country. Anne and her family felt safe once again.

Anne described the circumstances of her family's emigration years later in her diary: 'Because we're Jewish, my father immigrated to Holland in 1933, where he became the managing director of the Dutch Opekta Company, which manufactures products used in making jam.'

After years of enduring anti-Semitism in Germany, the Franks were relieved to once again enjoy freedom in their new hometown of Amsterdam. 'In those days, it was possible for us to start over and to feel free,' Otto recalled.

Anne began attending Amsterdam's Sixth Montessori School in 1934, and throughout the rest of the 1930s, she lived a relatively happy and normal childhood. Frank had many friends, Dutch and German, Jewish and Christian, and she was a bright and inquisitive student.

Adolf Hitler

The name of Adolf Hitler has a very special place in the pages of history. He was a man with a magnetic personality and sharp leadership and oratory skills. However, he used all these skills not for the betterment of the world but to kill and plunder people.

Hitler was the leader of Germany from 1933 to 1945. He was leader of the Nazi party, who rose to become the most powerful dictator in the world. His policies were known to precipitate World War II by invading Poland

and then invading many other European countries. Hitler is also well known for his plans to exterminate the Jewish people in the holocaust.

Hitler was born on April 20, 1899 in a city named Braunau am Inn in the country of Austria. He was the fourth of six children born to Alois Hitler and Klara Polzl. Hitler had a rather unhappy childhood as both his parents died fairly young and many of his brothers and sisters also passed away at short intervals.

As a young boy, Hitler did not fare well in his studies. He was expelled from a couple of schools before he moved to Vienna, Austria, to pursue his dream of becoming an artist. While living in Vienna, Hitler found that he did not have much artistic talent. Out of money, he moved into a homeless shelter, where he remained for several years.

When World War I began, Hitler joined the German army. He was awarded twice with the Iron Cross for bravery. It was during the war that Hitler became a strong German patriot and also came to love war.

After the war, Hitler entered politics. Many Germans were upset that they had lost the war. They were also opposed to the Treaty of Versailles, which not only put the blame of the war on Germany, but also took land away from Germany. At the same time, Germany was in an economic depression. Many people were poor. Between the depression and the Treaty of Versailles, the time was ripe for Hitler to rise to power.

Hitler entered politics only to discover that he was gifted in giving speeches, which began attracting regular audiences. People believed in what he said. Hitler soon joined the Nazi Party and rose to become its leader. He promised the people of restoring Germany to greatness in Europe. In 1933, he was elected the Chancellor of Germany.

After becoming the Chancellor, there was no looking back for Hitler. He had studied his idol, Benito Mussolini of Italy, and learnt how to install a fascist government and become a dictator. Shortly thereafter, Hitler used his position as Chancellor to form a de facto legal dictatorship.

In order for Germany to grow, Hitler thought the country needed more land or 'living space'. He first annexed

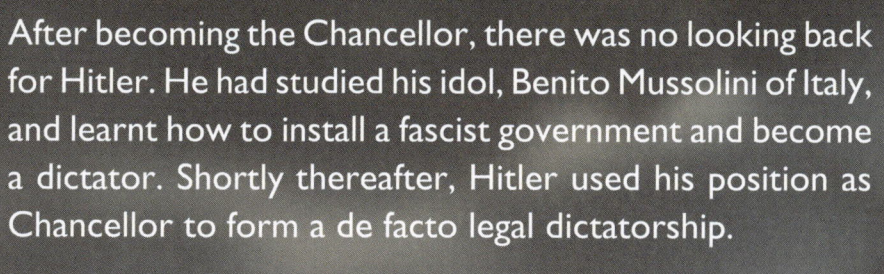

Austria as part of Germany and then took over part of Czechoslovakia. As though this weren't enough, on September 1, 1939, Germany invaded Poland, thus initiating World War II. Hitler formed an alliance with the Axis Powers of Japan and Italy, who were fighting the Allied Powers of Britain, France, the Soviet Union, and the United States.

Hitler's army began to take over much of Europe. They attacked quickly in what was called Blitzkrieg or 'lightning war'. Soon Germany had captured most of Europe including France, Denmark and Belgium. However,

the Allies fought back. On June 6, 1944, they invaded the beaches of Normandy and soon liberated France. By March of 1945, the Allies had defeated much of the German army. Afraid of falling into the hands of enemy troops, Hitler committed suicide on April 30, 1945.

Hitler was responsible for some of the most horrible crimes committed ever in human history. He hated the Jewish people and wanted to exterminate them from Germany. He forced the Jews to flee to concentration camps where 6 million Jews were killed during World War II. He also killed other people and races he did not approve of, not sparing even the handicapped.

Hitler's Heartless Treatment of the Jews

World War II commenced with the invasion of Poland by Germany in September 1939. Soon after, in 1940, the Nazis began establishing ghettos for the Jews of Poland. More than 10 percent of the Polish population was Jewish, numbering about 3 million. The Jews were forcibly deported from their homes to live in crowded ghettos, isolated from the rest of society.

The ghettos lacked the necessary food, water, space, and sanitary facilities required by so many people living within their constricted boundaries. Many died of deprivation and starvation. The Jews were also taken to gas chambers and killed in large groups.

This was known as 'holocaust', in which approximately 6 million Jews were killed in Hitler's regime.

In nearly every country overrun by the Nazis, the Jews were forced to wear badges marking them as Jews. They were rounded up into ghettos or concentration camps and then gradually transported to the killing centres. The death camps were essentially factories for murdering the Jews. The Germans shipped thousands of Jews to them each day. Within a few hours of their arrival, the Jews would be stripped of their possessions and valuables,

gassed to death, and their bodies burned in specially designed crematoriums. Approximately 3.5 million Jews were murdered in these death camps.

Many healthy, young, strong Jews were not killed immediately; instead, they were forced to work in German munitions and other factories.

The Franks' Hideout

On May 10, 1940, the German army invaded the Netherlands, defeating the Dutch forces after just a few days of fighting. The Dutch surrendered on May 15, 1940, marking the beginning of the Nazi occupation of the Netherlands.

As Anne later wrote in her diary, 'After May 1940, the good times were few and far between; first there was the war, then the capitulation and then the arrival of the Germans, which is when the trouble started for the Jews.'

Beginning in October 1940, the Nazi occupiers imposed anti-Jewish measures on the Netherlands. Jews were

forced to wear a yellow Star of David at all times. They were also forbidden from owning businesses. Anne and her sister were forced to join a segregated Jewish school. Otto managed to keep control of his company by officially signing ownership over to two of his Christian associates—Jo Kleiman and Victor Kugler—while continuing to run the company from behind the scenes.

Anne later wrote, 'I can remember that as early as 1932, groups of Storm Troopers came marching by, singing, "When Jewish blood splatters from the knife."' When Hitler became Chancellor of Germany on January 20, 1933, the Frank family immediately realized that it was time to flee. Otto later said, "Though this did hurt me deeply, I realized that Germany was not the world, and I left my country forever."

On June 12, 1942, Anne's parents gave her a red chequered diary for her 13th birthday. She wrote her first entry, addressed to an imaginary friend named Kitty, the same day, 'I hope I will be able to confide everything to you, as I have never been able to confide in anyone, and I hope you will be a great source of comfort and support.'

Weeks later, on July 5, 1942, Margot received an official summon to report to a Nazi work camp in Germany.

The very next day, the family went into hiding in makeshift quarters in an empty space at the back of Otto's company building. They referred to it as the 'Secret Annex'. They were accompanied in hiding by Otto's business partner Hermann van Pels as well as his wife, Auguste, and son, Peter. Otto's employees Kleiman and Kugler, as well as Jan and Miep Gies and Bep Voskuijl, provided food and information to the family about the outside world on a regular basis.

The time when they actually left their home in Amsterdam to head towards the hideout was a difficult one. Many final arrangements needed to be made and a few extra bundles of supplies and clothes needed to be taken to the Secret Annex ahead of their arrival.

They spent the afternoon packing but then had to remain quiet and seem normal around their upstairs renter until he finally went to bed. Around 11 p.m., Miep and Jan Gies arrived to take some of the packed supplies to the Secret Annex.

At 5:30 a.m. on July 6, 1942, the Frank family dressed in numerous layers so as to take a few extra garments with them without having to cause suspicion on the streets by carrying a suitcase. They left food on the counter, stripped the beds, and left a note giving instructions about who would take care of their cat.

Margot was the first to leave the apartment; she left on her bike. The rest of the Frank family left on foot at 7:30 a.m.

Anne had been told that there was a hiding place but not its location until the day of the actual move. The Frank family arrived safely at the Secret Annex, located in Otto's business premises at 263 Prinsengracht in Amsterdam.

Seven days later (July 13, 1942), the van Pels family (the van Daans in the published diary) arrived at the Secret Annex.

On November 16, 1942, Friedrich 'Fritz' Pfeffer (called Albert Dussel in the diary) became the last one to arrive.

The eight people hiding in the Secret Annex in Amsterdam never left their hiding place until the fateful day of August 4, 1944 when they were discovered and arrested.

Anne was 15 years of age when the family was found and sent to the camps, where she died of typhus.

The families spent two years in hiding, never once stepping outside the dark, damp, sequestered portion of the building. Since they could not go out, to kill time, Anne wrote extensive daily entries in her diary. Some of her entries betrayed the depth of despair into which she occasionally sunk during her stay in confinement. 'I've reached the point where I hardly care whether I live or die,' she wrote on February 3, 1944. 'The world will keep on turning without me, and I can't do anything to change events anyway.'

The entries that Anne wrote in her diary actually helped her to maintain her sanity and her spirits. 'When I write, I can shake off all my cares,' she wrote on April 5, 1944.

Along with her diary, Anne also filled a notebook with quotes from her favourite authors, original stories and the beginnings of a novel about her time in the Secret Annex. Her writings reveal a teenage girl with creativity, wisdom, depth of emotion and rhetorical power far beyond her years.

Captured by the Nazis

On August 4, 1944, a German secret police officer accompanied by four Dutch Nazis stormed into the Secret Annex, arresting everyone who was hiding there. They had been betrayed by an anonymous person, and the identity of their betrayer remains unknown to this day. The residents of the Secret Annex were shipped off to Camp Westerbork, a concentration camp in the northeastern Netherlands, and they arrived by passenger

train on August 8, 1944. They were transferred to the Auschwitz death camp in Poland in the middle of the night on September 3, 1944. Upon arriving at Auschwitz, the men and women were separated. This was the last time that Otto ever saw his wife or daughters.

After several months of hard labour hauling heavy stones and grass mats, Anne and Margot were again transferred during the winter to the Bergen-Belsen concentration

camp in Germany. Their mother was not allowed to go with them. Soon, Edith Frank fell ill and died at Auschwitz on January 6, 1945.

At Bergen-Belsen, food was scarce, sanitation was awful and disease ran rampant. Anne and her sister both contracted typhus in the early spring and died within a day of each other sometime in March 1945, just a few weeks before British soldiers liberated the camp. Anne was just 15 years old at the time of her death, and one of more than 1 million Jewish children who died in the camp.

Otto was the only member of the family to survive. At the end of the war, he returned home to Amsterdam, searching desperately for the news of his family. On July 18, 1945, he met two sisters who had been with Anne and Margot at Bergen-Belsen; they delivered the tragic news of their death.

The Diary of a Young Girl

When Otto returned to Amsterdam, he found Anne's diary, which had been saved by Miep Gies. He eventually gathered the strength to read it and was awestruck by what he discovered. 'There was revealed a completely different Anne to the child that I had lost,' Otto wrote in a letter to his mother. 'I had no idea of the depths of her thoughts and feelings.'

Otto was so touched by the contents of his daughter's diary that he decided to get them published as a book. So, The Secret Annex: Diary Letters from June 14, 1942

to August 1, 1944 was published on June 25, 1947. "If she had been here, Anne would have been so proud," he said. The *Diary of a Young Girl,* as it is typically called in English, has since been published in 67 languages. Countless editions, as well as screen and stage adaptations, of the work have been created around the world. The Diary of a Young Girl remains one of the most moving and widely read first-hand accounts of the Jewish experience during the holocaust.

Anne's diary endures, not only because of the remarkable events she described, but due to her extraordinary gifts as a storyteller and her indefatigable spirit through even the most horrific of circumstances. For all its passages of despair, Anne's diary is essentially a story of faith, hope and love in the face of hate. 'It's utterly impossible for me to build my life on a foundation of chaos, suffering and death,' she wrote on July 15, 1944. 'I see the world being slowly transformed into a wilderness; I hear the approaching thunder that, one day, will destroy us too. I feel the suffering of millions. And yet, when I look up at the sky, I somehow feel that everything will change for the better, that this cruelty too shall end, that peace and tranquility will return once more.'

In 2009, the Anne Frank Centre USA launched a national initiative called the Sapling Project, planting saplings from a 170-year-old chestnut tree that Anne had long loved (as denoted in her diary) at 11 different sites nationwide.

Excerpts from the Diary of Anne Frank

Tuesday, 22 December 1942

Oh, I'm becoming so sensible! We've got to be reasonable about everything we do here; studying, listening, holding our tongues, helping others, being kind, making compromises and I don't know what else! I'm afraid my common sense, which was in short supply to begin with, will be used up too quickly and I won't have any left by the time the war is over.

Wednesday, 13 January 1943

Terrible things are happening outside. At any time of night and day, poor helpless people are being dragged out of their homes. They're allowed to take only a rucksack and a little cash with them, and even then, they're robbed of these possessions on the way. Families are torn apart; men, women and children are separated. Children come home from school to find that their parents have disappeared. Women return from shopping to find their houses sealed, their families gone. The Christians in Holland are also living in fear because their sons are being sent to Germany. Everyone is scared. Every night hundreds of planes pass over Holland on their way to German cities, to sow their bombs on German soil. Every hour hundreds, or maybe even thousands, of people are being killed in Russia and Africa. No one can keep out of the conflict, the entire world is at war, and even though the Allies are doing better, the end is nowhere in sight.

I could spend hours telling you about the suffering the war has brought, but I'd only make myself more miserable. All we can do is wait, as calmly as possible, for it to end.

Saturday, 30 January 1943

Dearest Kitty,

I'm seething with rage, yet I can't show it. I'd like to scream, stamp my foot, give Mother a good shaking, cry and I don't know what else because of the nasty words, mocking looks and accusations that she hurls at me day after day, piercing me like arrows from a tightly strung bow, which are nearly impossible to pull from my body. I'd like to scream at Mother, Margot, the van Daans, Dussel and Father too: 'Leave me alone, let me have at least one night when I don't cry myself to sleep with my eyes burning and my head pounding. Let me get away, away from everything, away from this world!' But I can't do that. I can't let them see my doubts, or the wounds they've inflicted on me. I couldn't bear their sympathy or their good-humoured derision. It would only make me want to scream even more.

Everyone thinks I'm showing off when I talk, ridiculous when I'm silent, insolent when I answer, cunning when I have a good idea, lazy when I'm tired, selfish when I eat one bit more than I should, stupid, cowardly, calculating, etc., etc. All day long I hear nothing but what an exasperating child

I am, and although I laugh it off and pretend not to mind, I do mind. I wish I could ask God to give me another personality, one that doesn't antagonize everyone.

But that's impossible. I'm stuck with the character I was born with, and yet I'm sure I'm not a bad person. I do my best to please everyone, more than they'd ever suspect

in a million years. When I'm upstairs, I try to laugh it off because I don't want them to see my troubles.

Perhaps sometime I'll treat the others with the same contempt as they treat me. Oh, if only I could.

Sunday, 11 July 1943

It's not easy trying to behave like a model child with people you can't stand, especially when you don't mean a word of it. But I can see that a little hypocrisy gets me a lot further than my old method of saying exactly what I think.

Thursday, 29 July 1943

Dearest Kitty,

Mrs van Daan, Dussel and I were doing the washing-up and I was extremely quiet. This is very unusual for me and they were sure to notice, so in order to avoid any questions, I quickly racked my brains for a neutral topic.

Friday, October 29, 1943

My nerves often get the better of me, especially on Sundays; that's when I really feel miserable.

Saturday, October 30, 1943

I cling to Father because my contempt of Mother is growing daily and it's only through him that I'm able to retain the last ounce of family feeling I have left. He doesn't understand that I sometimes need to vent my feelings for Mother. He doesn't want to talk about it, and he avoids any discussion involving Mother's failings.

And yet Mother, with all her shortcomings, is tougher for me to deal with. I don't know how I should behave. I can't very well confront her with her carelessness, her sarcasm and her hard-heartedness, yet I can't continue to take the blame for everything.

Monday evening, November 8, 1943

If you were to read all my letters in one sitting, you'd be struck by the fact that they were written in a variety of moods. It annoys me to be so dependent on the moods here in the Annexe, but I'm not the only one; we're all subject to them. If I'm engrossed in a book, I have to rearrange my thoughts before I can mingle with other people, because otherwise they might think I was strange. As you can see, I'm currently in the middle of depression. I couldn't really tell you what set it off, but I think it stems from my cowardice, which confronts me at every turn. This evening, when Bep was still here, the doorbell rang long and loud. I instantly turned white, my stomach churned, and my heart beat wildly --and all because I was afraid.

At night in bed I see myself alone in a dungeon, without Father and Mother. Or I'm roaming the streets, or the Annexe is on fire, or they come in the middle of the night to take us away and I crawl under my bed in desperation. I see everything as if it were actually taking place. Sad to think it might all happen soon!

Friday, January 28, 1944

The best example of this is our own helpers, who have managed to pull us through so far and will hopefully bring us safely to shore, because otherwise they'll find themselves sharing the fate of those they're trying to protect. Never have they uttered a single word about the burden we must be, never have they complained that we're too much of trouble. They come upstairs every

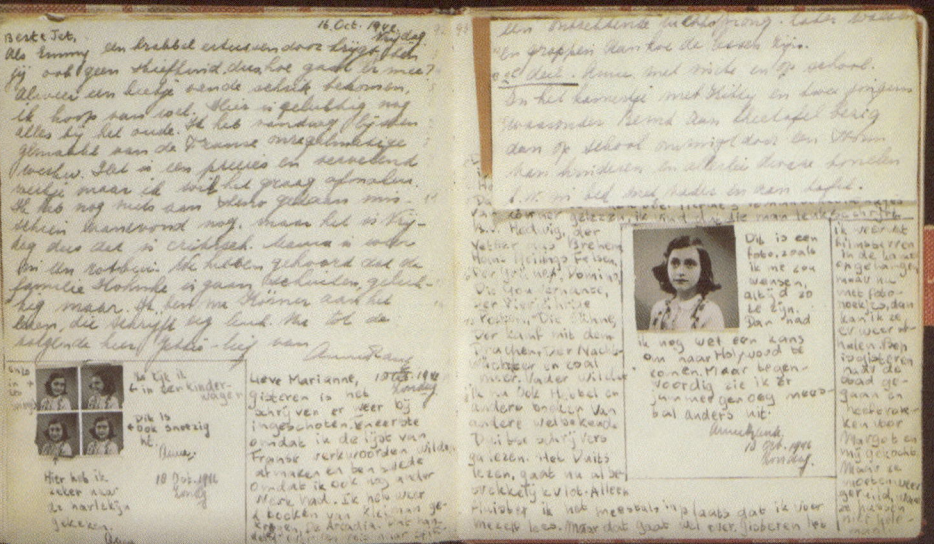

day and talk to the men about business and politics, to the women about food and wartime difficulties and top the children about books and newspapers. They put their most cheerful expressions, bring flowers and gifts for birthdays and special occasions and are always ready to do what they can. That's something we should never forget: while others display their heroism in battle or against the Germans, our helpers prove theirs every day by their good spirits and affection.

Thursday, February 3, 1944

All day long that's what I hear. Invasion, invasion, nothing but invasion. Arguments about going hungry, dying, bombs, fire extinguishers, sleeping bags, identity cards, poison gas, etc., etc. Not exactly cheerful... I'll just let matters take their course and concentrate on studying and hope that everything will be all right in the end.

Wednesday, February 23, 1944

But I also looked out of the open window, letting my eyes roam over a large part of Amsterdam, over the rooftops and on to the horizon, a strip of blue so pale it was almost invisible.

Tuesday, March 7, 1944

At such moments I don't think about all the misery, but about the beauty that still remains. This is where Mother and I differ greatly. Her advice in the face of melancholy is: 'Think about all the suffering in the world and be thankful you're not part of it. My advice is: 'Go outside, to the

country, enjoy the sun and all nature has to offer. Go outside and try to recapture the happiness within yourself; think of all the beauty in yourself and in everything around you and be happy'.

I don't think Mother's advice can be right, because what are you supposed to do if you become part of the suffering? You'd be completely lost. On the contrary, beauty remains, even in misfortune. If you just look for it, you discover more and more happiness and regain your balance. A person who's happy will make others happy; a person who has courage and faith will never die in misery!

Wednesday, May 3, 1944

There's a destructive urge in people, the urge to rage, murder and kill. And until all of humanity, without exception, undergoes a metamorphosis, wars will continue to be waged, and everything that has been carefully built up, cultivated and grown will be cut down and destroyed, only to start all over again!

I've often been down in the dumps, but never desperate. I look upon our life in hiding as an interesting adventure, full of danger and romance, and every privation as as amusing addition to my diary. I've made up my mind to lead a different life from other girls, and not to become an ordinary housewife later on. What I'm experiencing here is a good beginning to an interesting life, and that's the reason --the only reason-- why I have to laugh at the humorous side of the most dangerous moments.

I'm young and have many hidden qualities. I'm young and strong and living through a big adventure; I'm right in the middle of it and can't spend all day complaining because it's impossible to have any fun! I'm blessed with many things: happiness, a cheerful disposition and strength. Every day I feel myself maturing, I feel liberation drawing near, I feel the beauty of nature and the goodness of the people around me. Every day I think what a fascinating and amusing adventure this is! With all that, why should I despair?

Timeline

- **1929** Anne Frank is born on June 12, in Frankfurt, Germany to Otto Frank and Edith Frank

- **1933** Adolf Hitler becomes Chancellor of Germany and the first anti-Jewish laws are established

    The First Concentration Camp opens at Oranienburg outside Berlin Nazis boycott Jewish-owned shops.

    Nazis open Dachau concentration camp Otto and Edith Frank realize that they need to leave Germany and make plans to go to Holland

- **1934** Otto begins working at the Opekta Works and finds an apartment on the Merwedeplein (Merwede Square) in Amsterdam

    Edith, Margot and Anne leave Germany and join Otto in Amsterdam

    Anne Frank enrolls in a Montessori school in Amsterdam

    Adolf Hitler becomes Fuhrer or Chancellor of Germany

Timeline

- **1935** Germany passes the Nuremburg Race Laws that deprive German Jews of their citizenship, their businesses, and their right to education

- **1938** The United States and 32 other countries meet to discuss the growing Jewish refugee crisis but no country offers to take in Jewish refugees

- **1939** Germany invades Poland

    Britain, France, Austria and New Zealand declare War on Germany starting World War II

- **1940** The Germans invade and occupy the Netherlands

    The Germans order Jews to attend Jewish schools only, so Anne and her sister are enrolled at the Jewish Lyceum

- **1941** Dutch Jews are forbidden access to movie theatres and public transport, thus preventing Anne from enjoying her favourite pastime

    All Dutch Jews are forced to wear yellow stars

    The Japanese attack Pearl Harbor and

Timeline

           war is declared on the US

- 1942   Edith's mother, Rosa Holländer dies

    Anne receives an autograph book from her father for her birthday; she decides to use it as a diary

    Anne's older sister is ordered to report for relocation to a labour camp

    The Frank family go into hiding in Amsterdam because of Margot's deportation order; Anne has to leave behind her cat called Moortje

    Hermann van Pels (also known as Van Daan), Otto's partner, together with Auguste and 16-year-old Peter van Pels join the Frank family in the 'Secret Annex'.

    Fritz Pfeffer, a dentist and friend of the family, joins the annex

- 1943   The Germans surrender in the battle of Stalingrad and Germany starts retreating

- 1944   Anne makes her final entry in the diary

    The Secret Annex is stormed by the German Security Police; all of the residents of the annex are arrested and taken to the Gestapo headquarters where they are interrogated and held overnight

Everyone from the Secret Annex is sent to an overcrowded prison on the Weteringschans, where they stay for two nights

They are all sent in a cattle car to Auschwitz; once there, the men are separated from the women

Anne and Margot are transported to Bergen-Belsen concentration camp

■ 1945 Anne's mother, Edith Frank, dies of starvation at Auschwitz

The Russian Allies liberate the remaining survivors in Auschwitz, including Otto Frank

Margot dies of typhus in Bergen-Belson

Anne dies of typhus in Bergen-Belson

Hitler commits suicide

Germany surrenders to end World War II in Europe

Otto returns to Amsterdam, not knowing whether his family is still alive

Otto receives the news of his daughters' death at Bergen-Belsen; his friend Miep gives him the diary written by Anne that was found in the annex after the family was arrested.

- 1947 Anne's diary, *Anne Frank: Diary of a Young Girl,* is published in Amsterdam

Timeline

Research Work

Search the Internet to find out the following:

Who was Adolf Hitler?

What is holocaust?

Note down your information in a note pad or a file.

Diary Entry

Do you know how to write a diary? Write an entry about an eventful day in your life. Once you have noted down everything, share it in the class with your classmates and teacher.

Class Discussion

What is your idea of the two world wars? Discuss with your friends and your teacher. Also discuss the reasons for their outbreak, the destruction they caused and their outcome.

Questions

1. Who was Anne Frank?
2. Why is she remembered till this day?
3. Name her parents and her sister.
4. What do you understand by anti-semantic policy?

Activities

Activities

5. What is a holocaust?
6. Where was Anne born? Which religion did she follow?
7. How was Germany humiliated in World War I?
8. Name the government that came to power after the world war in Germany?
9. Who was Hitler?
10. How did he become the chancellor of Germany?
11. Who was Hitler inspired by?
12. Why did the Franks move out of Germany to Amsterdam?
13. What is a ghetto?
14. Why did the Frank family go into hiding?
15. When Anne was 13 years old, what did her father gift her?
16. Do you remember the date when Anne and her family were captured?
17. How did Anne, Margot and their mother die?
18. What did Anne write in her diary?
19. Why is diary so valuable till today?
20. What do you learn from the life of Anne?

Glossary

accusations: to charge that someone has done something illegal or wrong

adapted: to make something suitable for a new purpose

advantage: a condition that puts one in a favourable position

antagonize: to become unfriendly

anti-Semitic: unsympathetic to or prejudiced against Jews

betrayed: to give away information to an enemy

bravery: courageous behaviour

Chancellor: a senior state or legal official

chequered: a pattern of squares

churned: to shake milk or cream in a machine in order to get butter

circumstance: a fact that makes a situation the way it is

communists: people who support the principles of communism

compromise: an agreement or settlement of a dispute

concentration camps: a place in which large

Glossary

numbers of political prisoners are deliberately imprisoned in a relatively small area with inadequate facilities

confront: to come face to face with someone with hostile intentions

conservative: one who holds on to traditional values

crematorium: a place where a dead person's body is cremated

dedicated: devoted to a task or purpose

deport: to expel a foreigner from a country

deprivation: the damaging lack of material benefits

desperation: a state of despair, which results in rash behaviour

dictator: a ruler with total power over a country who has obtained control by force

disappear: out of sight

disrupt: to interrupt by causing a disturbance

dungeon: an underground prison cell as in a castle

economic depression: a long and severe recession in economy

Glossary

emigration: to leave one's own country to settle elsewhere permanently

encourage: to give support or confidence

engrossed: absorbed, involved or immersed

exasperating: intensely irritating

expel: to force out something or someone

exterminate: to destroy completely

extinguisher: a device used to put out fire

extraordinary: very unusual

fascist: a follower of the political philosophy called fascism

ghettos: a part of a city, especially a slum area, occupied by a minority group of people

handicapped: a person having restricted ability to function physically, mentally, or socially

holocaust: destruction on a mass scale, especially caused by fire or nuclear war

homosexual: people who are sexually attracted to people of one's own sex

humiliation: to feel insulted due to someone's words or actions

hypocrisy: to pretend to have higher standards

Glossary

impose: to force an unwelcome decision on someone

indefatigable: persisting tirelessly

inquisitive: showing an interest in learning about things

insolent: rude and arrogant

instability: the state of being unstable

invade: to enter a country or region with the intention of conquering it commit bound to a certain policy

isolated: far away from other places, buildings, or people

Jehovah: a form of the Hebrew name of God used in some translations of the Bible

Judaism: the religious and cultural traditions of the Jews

leadership: the ability to lead an organization or people

makeshift: acting as an interim and temporary measure

miserable: to be very unhappy

Montessori: a system of education for young

children through activities rather than through formal teaching methods

opponents: someone who competes with or opposes another in a contest or game

oratory: effective public speaking

persecution: ill-treatment of people because of race, political or religious beliefs

piercing: having keen intelligence

plunder: to steal goods from a place or person by using force

pounding: to strike something heavily in a repeated manner

reveal: to make previously unknown or secret information known to others

ridiculous: something that is strange or absurd

scholarly: relating to serious academic study

segregate: to set apart from the rest or from each other; isolate or divide

slaughter: to kill people or animals in a violent way in large numbers

starvation: suffering or death caused by lack of food

Glossary

traditions: long-established customs or beliefs that have been passed on from one generation to another

tranquil: free from disturbance

typhus: an infectious disease caused by rickettsiae, characterized by a purple rash, headaches, fever; also called spotted fever

unemployment: lack of occupation or means of earning